a Queen

through
my eyes

ALFONZO MCINTOSH

Edited by La Tasha Taylor (The Write Legacy 3 - thewritelegacy3@gmail.com)

Cover design by David James

ISBN: 978-0-578-87036-6

Printed in the United States of America

Dedication

———— ⦿ ————

First and foremost I would like to give honor and praise to my Lord and Savior Jesus Christ. I also dedicate this book to my loving wife La Trisha McIntosh. My loving mother, Terry McIntosh, and my daughter Sydney McIntosh. My foundations, Grandmother Adeline McIntosh, and Annie Dell Lee (May you continue to rest in heaven). And to all the beautiful women that have affected my life's journey.

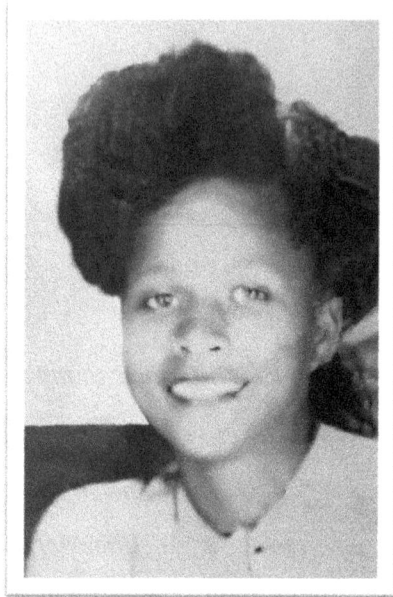

Adeline McIntosh

Annie Dell Lee

La Trisha McIntosh

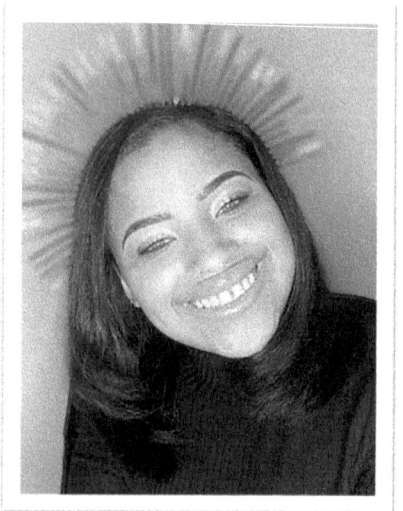

Sydney McIntosh

Contents

Introduction

───────── ✤ ─────────

This book is a glimpse of the poetic journey I am blessed to share with some extraordinary black women. Queens that I loved, queens that I admired, queens that I hurt, queens that nurtured a young boy into the man you see today. There are many beautiful women in this world, but none more beautiful than the one's I was blessed to see up close: My blood, My seed, My friend, My village, My love.

For You I Have Time

Born into creation, we birth this land. Walking next to the tall trees and the plush greens of the Serengeti, our love roamed. Eclipsing the mountain of Ethiopia, our bond reached heaven's gate. The love that this atmosphere created blinded us from the pitfalls that deceitfully waited. From the beginning of time, the enemy was always there to try to break what God had put together. But the enemy could not eclipse the words of our King, what God put together let no man put asunder. Taken to the land, we never knew; sown into a dream, we didn't sow. Our love continued to blossom through the hardships of time, like a beautiful rose escaping her thorns. Painfully we started the walk of this new journey looking into each other eyes for hope as the lash of a stinging whip tried to strike us down. I cried and sometimes died when you were taken from me in the middle of the night to be violated by a man who didn't know your true worth. For if he did, he would know he was violating the very essence of his existence. Yet we persevered, dancing and singing in our dreams while our nightmare slept beside us.

Years passed as our love continue to soar like an eagle above the fray as a Crow named Jim plucked at our wings to make us fall from grace. What could not be understood by the laws of the wicked was understood by you and me.

Being separated by the Crow was not a condemnation but a gift as it gave a King more time with his Queen. We created our own world in a world that was not meant to be ours. Through the pain of a noose tied to our neck hanging from a lifeless oak tree far gone from the Acacias of the Serengeti, we stood together.

In the struggle, we sat side by side at an Alabama lunch counter, fighting for the right to sit next to someone who didn't deserve our precious time, as we tried to get a morsel to eat from the white man's table. I lay next to you on a cold Chicago morning, being your covering as bullets blew into our room because we raised our fist to oppression. All of this happened before the sun rose. What they didn't know, the SON had already raised, and he was watching. We cried together as a war called crack infiltrated the veins of our community for political gain, trying to pull me away from you, as they told us to "Just Say No!" Through it all, we persevered. Standing strong together, we celebrated with joy when we saw one of our Kings leading our country at the head of a table where we once begged for crumbs. Our eyes set upon a queen raised from Mississippi's sweltering prejudice to become a billionaire inspiration that showed the little black girl's what life could be.

Through all the Good and bad to our love for each other, we held on. Now those times seem like a distant memory in a history book that has been closed. Seldom is a King seen covering his Queen. When we sit side by side, we look at each other with envy and jealousy, making it seem that there is no room for both of us at a table prepared for us. The hate that came from without is now embedded within, eating away at our soul worse than any skin that is not our own could ever do. Black love is a metaphor, a figure of speech that, when spoken of, is met with all love matters, when in the past it only mattered to us. But to this, my eyes are not blind. This King still sees his Queen.

From birth, a son recognized you as you held me in the warmth of your arms. Nurturing me with your love, and as a husband, I looked into my own queens' eyes and committed for a lifetime. As a Father, I held a future Queen teaching, guiding her for a future King. Although the world has forgotten, my history book will never be closed. For you and our story, I will always have time.

Be Still

Lying beside you, I look at a perfect creation from God above. Skin glowing in your almond tone, lips perfected by a seed of mankind, a nose that inhales and exhales the beauty inside. As your love curls beneath my heart. I just want you to be still—a request simple in tone, complex in nature. Scrolling the history of your pain, I open your book of life. Seeing, what these beautiful eyes were not meant to see by the thoughts of man but were required by God to bring your love to me. Opening the door of hurt, I look beyond the veil of a Queen's smile, hiding the girl wounded by life's movement beyond her control.

Rejection consumed her young mind as she insulated herself in frustration with her book of life. Beyond the make-up of a young woman scorned, cracks reveal themselves of broken promises and crushed dreams. Yet she presses on toward the mark of the high calling, knowing that it is not God that has forsaken her. Attempts to move on from a place of heartache. She opens herself up again to a new land of promise, but she did not understand pain travels with baggage that could not be detected—the pain of a different form. But of the same mind. Unknowingly she grabbed hold of it wholeheartedly, making a seed of her own. Now the pain was not just her own. Life came too soon with no way out; now, she was left alone. Alone with the scars that healing could not reach. Then with God's mercy, your pain found my pain to be healed in God's hands. Yet still, completion can only be perfected through the fire, as my own baggage tried to reopen the door of a pain that was so vehemently shut closed. But the prayers of the righteous availeth much, as the fire purified us instead of destroying. It gave me another chance to be the cupbearer of a heart screaming to be held. That's why as you lay beside me, all I want you to do is be still, still in my love for you—never wanting hurt to reach you again.

A Letter to My Mom

Thinking of a note to sing, an out of tune sound is the only thing that can orchestrate my thoughts of you. Realizing no sound explains the beautiful love ballad that your heart sings daily to my life. Putting together a perfect word to speak to you, my pen lays motionless, reaching from the depths of my soul only to finally comprehend there are no words that could pass my lips that can reach you to begin to explain what you mean to me.

The first woman I loved unconditionally, you are. You were the first person that showed me what friendship can truly be, knowing that I could always confide in you. From the first moment I recognized love, I recognized you — knowing your love was true to me. Released from your womb, you cradled me in your arms, never letting go until you instilled the man in me.

When I fell back in my cradle of sin, you picked me up, dusted me off, and said, son, God still has the plan for your life; it's in your hands. From that moment, I held onto those words for dear life, knowing that every word you spoke to me was in truth.

You showed me what a woman should be; that's why I have a woman as sweet as you next to me. I write these words to remind myself of the joy you bring to my life and give your flowers to you while your light still shines bright. The love I speak to you is infinity because your love has no end from my beginning.

Sunshine

—————❦—————

Looking into your eyes as I cradled you in my arms, I stood mesmerized, scared, and in awe at the gift God gave a flawed man. Bright as the sun, adorable as they come, your eyes took hold of me, searching for the Father you needed me to be. It was a daunting task for a man still searching for what life was supposed to be. Yet and still, I leaped forward with open arms, stumbling while trying to guide you in a dark world without spiritual light. It was, at times, an awkward affair. But it didn't matter; I had the joy of my life. You were meant for me as I was meant for you with the clarity I spoke. But clarity did not always speak back to me as I looked in the mirror of a broken man; my deep-rooted flaws are shown to me. It hindered our love from being complete. You were scorned without me even knowing.

Not realizing the pain I caused another would be the pain I caused you. Yet you remained cradled in my arms, mending a broken soul back together. You did not give up on me, holding on to the man you wanted me to be. As you grew in age, I grew in the spirit of a

Father. I was learning to nurture where I had not been—giving my heart completely, which before had seemed so foreign to me. We grew in love, what God intended to be.

I could never explain my love for you properly, but with these words, I try. But with these words, I try. My heart begins and ends with the thought of you. Every step that I now take is a path for you to become the woman God intended you to be. I live for the Sunshine you bring to me. No weapon formed against you shall prosper; with my Savior, I come into agreement. Spread your wings, daughter, and follow God's lead. Your promises are greater than your circumstance is a prophetic word I speak. Black Queen rise is what a father speaks as my FATHER speaks to me. From my rocky beginning with you, I can now see our beautiful ending—my Sunshine.

Sunday Morning

Like a Sunday Morning, my soul rests with the thought of you. The smell of bacon crackling on a stovetop, while a spiritual hymn breathes out from the beautiful soul that rests in you. A subtle smile that made a young boy's "peace be still" reminds me of you. Trouble seems to relinquish itself when I was near you. Wisdom of our God spoke through you. A testament to the times as you labored in love to make my joy complete. When I was a child, I spoke as a child, but you did not hold it against me. With a tone of grace, you spoke life into me. Simple words, stand up taller, speak clearer, listen harder. I took these words and more to heart putting away childish things growing into a man you knew I could be. There is so much I owe that I could never repay you, as I sit here still and calm like Sunday Morning thinking of you. You affected me without even knowing what was meant to be. Raising and nurturing a seed that birthed me, you walked in a prophetic word of a generation to come. From the moment I laid eyes on you, I was captured in your rapture of love. Although time has taken you away from me, in me, your work will always remain. Whether in memory or from a distance, you will always be my Sunday Morning.

A Woman Without a Title

Standing to a mother's side, you looked in love and admiration at a seed that was not your own. Cherishing the moment a village could begin to raise me, you stood in anticipation, grasping the time taking me in your arms, behind a door locked with your heart. A woman without a title gazed into my eyes like I was the only one in this world. Your motto spoken was no child left behind, but I was made to feel like the only child left. A pinched cheek, a playful chase, an adoring hug, a cheerful conversation, a bite to eat were the simple yet most important things to a boy trying to find his place in a world, a place that could sometimes seem cold and dark to a child's heart. Even when my childish ways turned into something your eyes were not meant to see, you embraced me with the wisdom of a mother, not my own. When my own needed rest, you gave her a pillow of time to ease a troubled mind. Sometimes love became blurry as I looked at your love above my mother's adoration. You quickly gave me the vision to see how truly special my mother's love was to me — knowing from experience the daunting task that motherhood could be, a woman without a title was your name, but it could never explain what you meant to me.

Remember the Time

I reminisce of times past. Remember the time when innocence is all boy and girl had. Hearing the chopping sounds of skates on the hardened concrete as we raced through life hand in hand. Your warm smile made a cold world feel innocent to a young man needing acceptance; your laughter put his mind at ease. Remember the time we ran the amazing race together? If it was only from the church to the storefront, it seemed like forever in a moment. You won the race, but after I got over the pain of defeat, I realized I was just happy to be in your space. Remember the time we made each other our therapist as you poured your heart out to me and I to you, crying and laughing over the frailties of love.

We both saw each other's hidden scars of past relationships as we clumsily tried to heal them with our naive words.

We did not choreograph our relationship; our relationship choreographed us as we danced to our own beat. I felt your pain; you felt mine. I saw your heartbeat for me; you saw my heart beat for you.

There was no other way; this is what God intended it to be. We played together, prayed together, argued together, laughed until the risen sun, and cried under an eclipsed moon. You were my sister without a womb. Taking for granted times past, I sit here embracing you in thought, looking from a distance seeing how you've grown. A girl, a young lady, A Black Queen now standing on her own.

Heaven Knows

Strength, wisdom, understanding, calm in a storm, prayer in chaos, love when hatred stomps at the doorstep.

Heaven knows what a world needs even before its eyes were open to see. A woman ordinary could not touch. A Queen a crown could not cover, a position filled by God above. Standing in a crowd, you stood alone in my eyes. In a gaze, I wondered at the extraordinary gift my savior had laid before me. As I could not understand, I only react affectionately to the love you showed. I sometimes selfishly just wanted it for me, but your reach was far beyond what my eyes could see A stamp of God's grace was put on everything you touched. But what you touched did not always give God's grace back to you. It did not matter your heart was above reproach. A love with no limits. A heart with no defect. Time was the only thing that could hinder you, as your light flickered away from me. But that was only a vague view. Your light was never gone; it was and will always be in full view, written in the book of God's glory.

His light will forever shine through you. Her name is not forgotten; her name is written. Annie Dell Lee, Erma Jean Newsome, Katy Mae Lee, Eddie Mae Crummie, Verlene Williams, Shaunita Brown, Tina Wallace, Rosie Macon, Yvonne Young, Nancy Slaughter, Lydia Powell, Naomi Whittington, Catherine Austin, Lucile Jones, Linda Evans, and all the other numerous women that shined there light upon me.

I Cry

―――――∽∞∾―――――

As God raised you from my side, I slept dreaming of the thought of you. God's creation, a masterpiece, a work of art, a Queen made just for me. Awaken, I realized you were more than what my thoughts could be. The Flesh of my Flesh, Bone of my Bone, we were one. Without you, there would be no me. From the beginning of time, I marveled at the blessing God bestowed upon me. I was at peace in the presence of your creation. Nothing could come between what God had put together except me, as a carnal mind created a devil's work. Taking my eyes off God's prize, I allowed sin to inflict a wound on our hearts, taking us from a garden of love to the reality of self-inflicted pain.

My first fail, but it would not be my last. I inflicted my carnal ways upon my black queen through centuries, decades, years, days, minutes, and seconds. Lust, deceit, selfishness, lies, anger engulfed me, suffocating the love that struggled to keep the embrace we shared. I cry, thinking of the pain I caused you. You were meant to play as my A-side, but a B-side is the only tune I allowed you to hear.

21

We were supposed to walk side by side; instead, I put you to the side as a waste to my vanity. I gazed into those beautiful brown eyes, but they were not yours I longed for; trying to walk like a man, I found myself only playing the game of a child, stomping on your emotions without consequence, or so I thought.

I consequently lost everything as I walked away, gaining nothing— an empty soul, without his flesh or bone. I cry, but you smile, for you are strong. God's creation is for the world to see and not just for me. To see the possibilities that I could not, and feel the love that I rejected at all cost. Hear the wisdom that I cut off. Your smile was too deep for me. You smile because you will forever remain a queen, even if it's not for me.

Pretty Brown Eyes

The streets beat through her heart, clouds of smoke rise through her lungs as the color red seeps into her eyes, disguising the pretty brown eyes that have captivated me. Her mind searches the cracked mirror of her reflection. Looking at a girl from years past that has been broken.

Broken dreams, broken promises, broken men have cultivated her body into concrete, blocking out the love that I' seek. Pretty Brown eyes open up only slightly for me to see what her love could truly be. Her eyes penetrate my uncultivated thoughts. Her lips stimulate the pulse of fresh blood rushing to my heart that pounds for her touch. Her curves wrap around my desires to penetrate her softness; she gives me a glimpse of ever so briefly.

Pretty Brown eyes have put a stronghold on this young heart. Some say that I'm a fool. They speak of the Pretty Brown eyes as a snare to my naïve ways. They say the concrete that holds her can never be broken. Violence fills her path. Anger choreographs her life; street life fills her cup. But this does not matter to me. Where they see violence, I see someone fighting to live. When they speak of her anger, I see no one showing her the love I can give as they show me her street life. I go beyond the exterior and look inside to see a fragile soul trying to survive a cold world. Yes, this may all be a façade to a young man trying to find his way. But every time I look into those Pretty Brown eyes, that's a chance I'm willing to take.

Intimate Thoughts

The sheet that covers my heart;

    the pillow that comforts my thoughts — you are.

In the bed of romance, we lay, surrounded by candles

    of love, trust, and communication.

We let the passion start from within,

    never letting lust be our trust,

    for, in God, we trusted.

I look into your eyes and beyond;

    I see the soul of a beautiful spirit.

I look at your lovely face and beyond;

    I see a beautiful mind that has captured my thoughts.

I look at your breasts and beyond;

    I see a pure heart that only beats for me.

I look at your thighs and beyond;

    I see the desire that only runs to me.

A QUEEN THROUGH MY EYES

I now realize that intimate thoughts

    can lay with God's thoughts.

I realize lust can be nurtured in love, as long as it's captured

    in a picture-perfect frame created by God above.

I walked, lost as your Adam, in my garden of sin,

    lost and confused;

    and then you came, created as my Eve to be by my side.

But in this true story, we did not sin,

    as you fed me fruit that I needed,

    and not what I wanted.

The fruit of love, commitment, honesty, and passion.

Now, I stand here, in love with you,

    thinking intimate thoughts,

    only true loves can share.

Naked

Stripped of every hurt and every pain;

I stand, naked, before your love,

    exposed for the world to see my heart beats in a beautiful,

      rhythmic symphony for your love

Thoughts of you run, naked, in my Garden of Eden,

      where there is only you and me, and the God we serve

Happiness has come to me in a time that I thought

      it would always be a distant love to me

Trust has shown me that everything

You are it is truth to me.

Communication whispered in my ear,

I could finally take off the clothes of a closed mind

    that should have never belonged to me

Naked, I stand before you,

      because this is what you have shown me;

for without your nakedness,

every private part of me could not be exposed.

I stand, in serenity; I walk in peace;

I laugh in bliss; I cry in joy;

I talk in the love you have exposed to me.

www.ingramcontent.com/pod-product-compliance
Lightning Source LLC
Chambersburg PA
CBHW071941020426
42331CB00010B/2968